Inspirational Thoughts
and Prayers

FOR EACH NEW DAY

A Collection of Inspirational Thoughts, Verses,
Poetry, Prayers and Scriptures
to Bless You Each New Day

Compiled by
Noah S. Martin

Companion Press
P.O. Box 310
Shippensburg, PA 17257-0310

ISBN 1-56043-529-1

109 South St.
Johnstown, PA 15901
Phone (814) 535-8202

Sponsorships of This Book

The publication of this book has been made possible by the financial support of the persons listed below. Grateful appreciation is expressed for their generosity and prayerful support.

Everett and Mary Hilliard
Lewis and Betty Lou James
Frank and Judy Treece
James E. Loveridge
Vern and Deb Henry
Rick and Karen Martin
Charlotte Ellis
Noah and Sandy Martin

In Loving Memory

Larry and Linda Blackburn in loving memory of daughter, Lori Blackburn

Charles and Myrna Gilbert in loving memory of father, John G. Schuliger

Terry and Lois Gilbert in loving memory of parents, V. Merle and Gladys Stewart

Lois Ringgold in loving memory of husband, Carroll Ringgold

In Honor

Terry and Lois Gilbert in honor of parents, Don and Henrietta Gilbert

This book is dedicated to —

- the many faithful and loyal supporters of the New Day ministry since its beginnings in 1978 to the present time
- the many individuals and families who entrusted New Day with their problems and demonstrated with great courage that each new day is an opportunity to begin anew
- the many New Day volunteers who have given themselves for the mission of the Lord Jesus Christ
- the dedicated members of the staff of New Day
- the dedicated members of the Board of Directors
- the dedicated members of Friends of New Day
- the dedicated trustees of New Day's Charitable Trust
- the many churches and pastors for their prayers, encouragement and support
- the honor and glory of the Lord Jesus Christ who loved us and gave Himself for us that we might know the joy of our salvation

Contents

Introduction

Day by day you live out your life. There is the first day and the last day—"a time to be born and a time to die"—and a great number of days in between. Some days are filled with sunshine, brightness and joy; other days are stormy, filled with darkness, despair and grief. But each day the presence of God is with you to bless you, guide you, comfort you, and encourage you. His love for you is new every morning.

Each new day is an opportunity to know God and to be with Him. You were not created just to endure life on this earth and to barely eke it through each day, waiting around to be rescued "in the sweet bye and bye."

You were created to be with Him today and to walk in His presence. Today is the day of salvation. Today is the day to move on from the past, forgetting those things which are behind, forgiving and being forgiven, pressing on into the new things God is preparing for you. For where He is you may be also—beginning now! You have already been raised with Christ and made to sit with Him in the heavenly places (Ephesians 2:4-6). The fellowship with Christ is now. The celebration is on! The table is spread! You are invited to come to the marriage feast, for everything is ready! (Matthew 22:1-4).

The promise of God-with-me each new day gives rise to many hopeful thoughts about life and its meaning. For example, I have dedicated much of my life working with people who are struggling with difficult issues. Many struggling people are ready to give up on life. They fear that life will always hurt. They see no hope for change. They feel betrayed and alone.

But there is hope! The God who created life in the beginning gives to life His continual creative power not only to sustain it, but also to change it and to recreate it, even to make new. The same creative power of God that established the earth and the heavens, the sun and the moon, the land and the sea, and all forms of life, including human, is active in the present moment to bring new life to your days.

Each new day brings you a powerful message: You are not alone! The Creator of your life is with you! You are not doomed to a life of pain and misery. "With God all things are possible!" (Matthew 19:26). "Behold, I make all things new" (Revelation 21:5) is a promise for you!

Your hope is this: the creative power of God can change your life, your world and your situations. The God who created the world out of nothing can create anew by His power. Hope happens when you apply the power of the living God to your situation.

The ministry of New Day, Inc. that serves troubled youths, marriages and families in Western Pennsylvania is based upon the belief that the creative power of God through Jesus Christ is present by His Holy Spirit to make new, to create, to recreate—to help broken people start over again. Each New Day represents the possibility of New Life if God is in it.

The Prologue

IN THE BEGINNING GOD CREATED THE HEAVENS AND THE EARTH.

— Genesis 1:1

And God said, "Let there be light";
and there was light.
And God saw that it was good;
and God separated the light from the darkness.
God called the light Day, and the darkness he called Night.
And there was
evening
and
morning,

ONE DAY.

— Genesis 1:3-5

I

The New Day

The Mighty One, God the Lord,
speaks and summons the earth
from the rising of the sun to its setting.

Psalm 50:1

Reach out in the early morning mist,
As the day's sun
Breaks the calmness of night,
And rise to the new day,
A new awareness of being.

Shake hands with the world,
And smile.

It's great to be alive!

jonivan

The Day Awakes

The day awakes,
  the morning breaks,
    the birds sing,
      the flowers open,
the earth springs to life
in your glorious sunshine.

So may I, O God, awake
  to the joy of your presence,
    sing a song of praise,
      open my heart to you,
        and spring to life
  in your glorious sunshine.
And in chorus with nature,
my soul rises to praise you.

Noah S. Martin

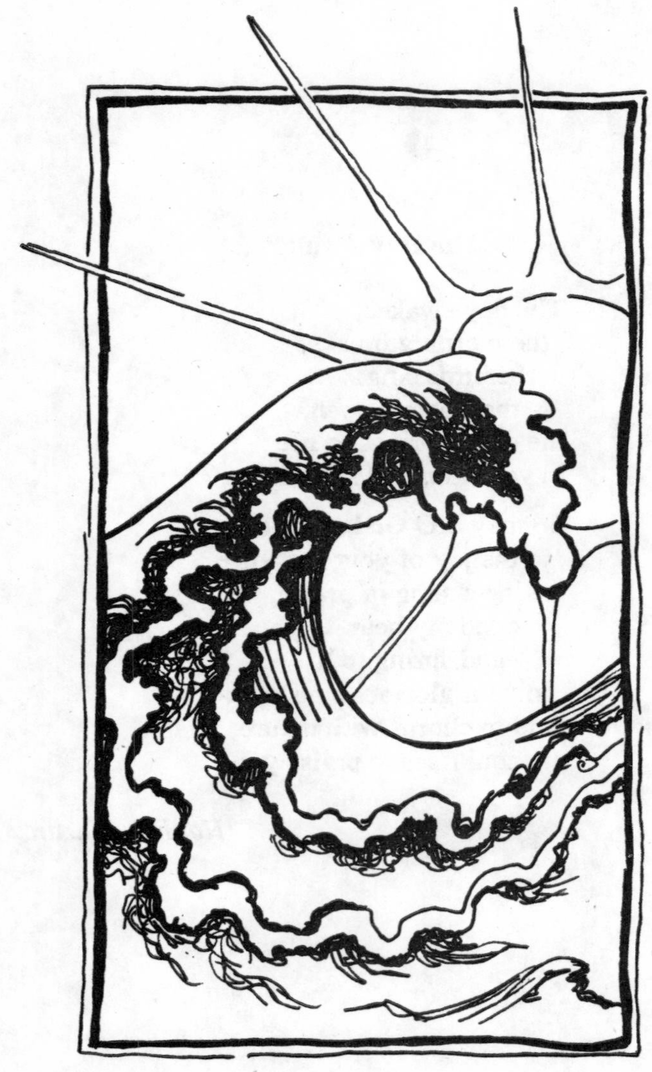

Today Is a New Day

Every morning is a fresh beginning. Every day is the world made new. Today is a new day.
Tomorrow is my world made new. I have lived all my life up to this moment, to come to this day.
This moment—this day—is as good as any moment in all eternity. I shall make of this day—each moment of this day—a heaven on earth.
This is my day of opportunity.

Dan Custer

Today is a day which we never had before,
which we shall never have again.
It rose from the great ocean of eternity,
and again sinks into its unfathomable depths.

Talmage

Morning Has Broken

Morning has broken like the first morning,
Blackbird has spoken like the first bird.
Praise for the singing, praise for the morning,
Praise for them springing fresh from the Word!

Sweet the rain's new fall, sunlit from heaven,
Like the first dewfall on the first grass.
Praise for the sweetness of the wet garden,
Spring in completeness where His feet pass!

Mine is the sunlight, mine is the morning,
Born of the one light Eden saw play.
Praise with elation, praise every morning,
God's recreation of the new day!

Eleanor Farjeon

There is a wonderful life waiting to be lived.
Celebrate it today; life is too short to
put off living until tomorrow.

Collin McCaty

II

Begin the Day With God

Every morning lean thine arms awhile
Upon the window sill of heaven
And gaze upon the Lord.
Then, with the vision in thy heart,
Turn strong to meet the day.

author unknown

Thou dost show me the path of life;
in thy presence there is fullness of joy,
in thy right hand are pleasures for evermore.
Psalm 16:11

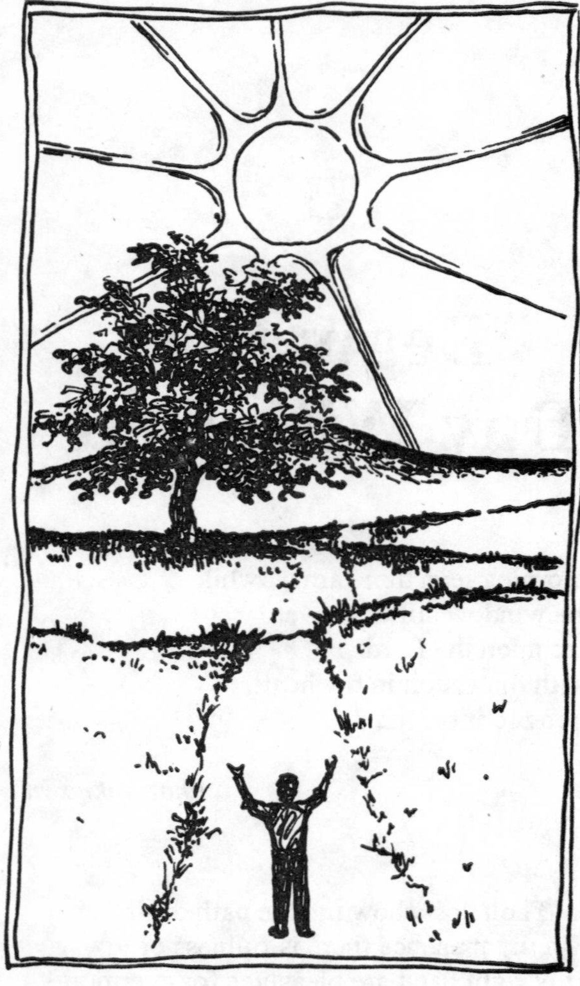

The Awakening

When the Light of Life falls upon the life
of men, secret powers begin to unfold,
sleeping perceptions begin to awake,
and the whole being becomes alive unto God.

John Henry Jowett

He who runs from God in the morning
will scarcely find him the rest of the day.

Bunyan

My presence will go with you,
and I will give you rest.
Exodus 33:14

The soul can split the sky in two,
And let the face of God shine through.

Edna St. Vincent Millay
from "Renascence"

Be strong and of good courage,
do not fear or be in dread...
For it is the Lord your God
who goes with you;
He will not fail you or forsake you.
Deuteronomy 31:6

The Secret

I met God in the morning
When my day was at its best,
And His presence came like sunrise,
Like a glory in my breast.

All day long the Presence lingered,
All day long He stayed with me,
And we sailed in perfect calmness
O'er a very troubled sea.

Other ships were blown and battered.
Other ships were sore distressed,
But the winds that seemed to drive them
Brought to us a peace and rest.

Then I thought of other mornings,
With a keen remorse of mind,
When I too had loosed the moorings,
With the presence left behind.

So I think I know the secret,
Learned from many a troubled way;
You must seek Him in the morning
If you want Him through the day!

Ralph Spaulding Cushman

III

The Miracle of a New Day

To me every hour of the light and dark is
a miracle,
Every cubic inch of space is a miracle.

Walt Whitman: Miracles, I. 17

Let all the earth fear the Lord,
let all the inhabitants of the world
stand in awe of him!
For he spoke, and it came to be;
he commanded, and it stood forth.
Psalm 33:8-9

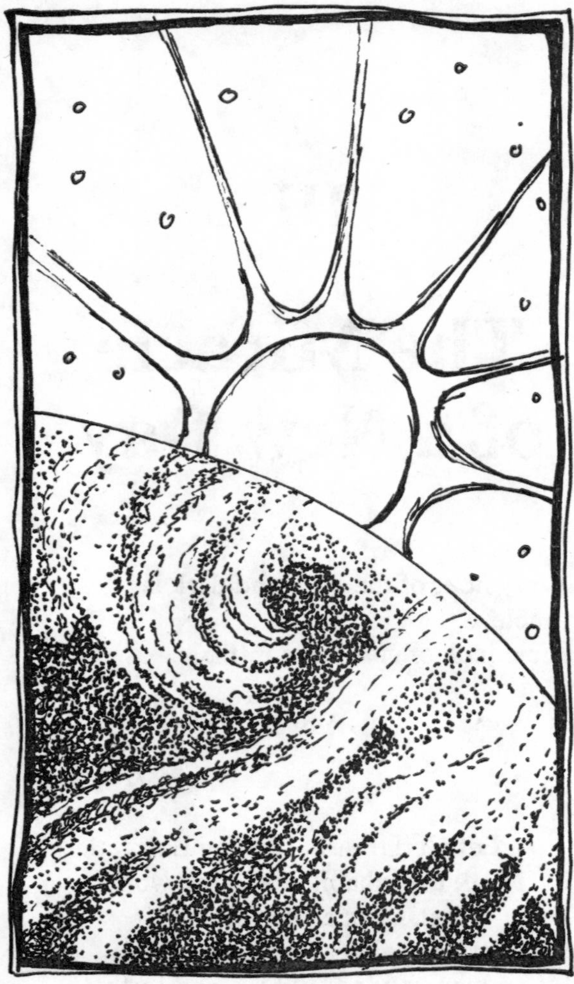

Each New Day Is a Miracle

Each New Day is a miracle from God!

It takes as great a miracle for each
New Day to begin as it took that first
day of creation when God said,
"Let there be light!"

The world is held together in such
precise detail that only the ongoing,
creative power of God from day to day
makes it possible.

This day is a precious gift from God!

Your life is a precious gift from God!

Therefore walk through this day humbly,
joyfully and graciously for you are
living in the midst of the awesome
presence of God the Creator who has
given you life that you may know Him
and love Him.

Noah S. Martin

Every moment of this strange and lovely life from dawn to dusk, is a miracle. Somewhere, always, a rose is opening its petals to the dawn. Somewhere, always, a flower is fading in the dusk. The incense that rises with the sun, and the scents that die in the dark, are all gathered, sooner or later, into the solitary fragrance that is God. Faintly, elusively, that fragrance lingers over all of us.

From *The Fool Hath Said* by Beverley Nichols

IV

The Gift of a New Day

Those precious gifts
Are yours and mine...
The sun, the moon,
The stars that shine,
And each new day
With all it holds,
Sunsets that glow
With reds and golds,
The flowers that bloom,
The showers that fall,
And life, the greatest
Gift of all!

Helen Farries

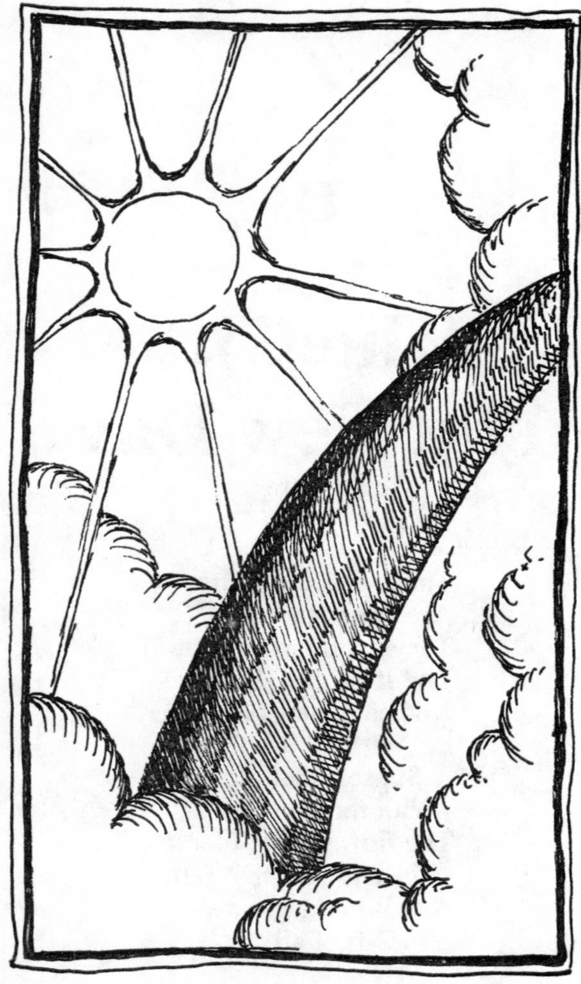

This Day Is a Gift from God

He has given us morning,
 Brightness and sun;
Food to be eaten
 And work to be done.
He has given us prayer
 With its wonderful power
To lighten our hearts
 In a troublesome hour.
He has given us rainbows,
 Flowers and song
And the hand of a dear one
 To help us along,
He has given us blessings
 To brighten our way;
And always—the gift
 Of another New Day.

Jean Kyler McManus

Thine is the day, thine also the night;
thou hast established the luminaries
and the sun.
Thou hast fixed all the bounds of the earth;
thou hast made summer and winter.

Psalm 74:16-17

A Precious Gift

This morning God gave me a precious gift—
A wonderful, unused day.
It is mine to use however I wish,
To use in my own special way.
Each yesterday, too, was an unused day
All clean, all sparkling, all mine;
But I filled them with regrets of the past
And dreams of future divine.
I don't live in those yesterdays
The life I would like to live.
The moments, the hours just slipped away
Like water through a sieve,
And left just nothingness behind,
I had won for God no soul—
Not one accomplishment,
No closer to life's goal.
Dear God, as I take this unused day
Help me to realize
It might be my last, I must use it well
Each moment I truly must prize.
Today is all we can live today;
Yesterday is but a dream.
Tomorrow is ever beyond our grasp;
A vision but dimly seen.
May I spend each golden moment well
That tomorrow will hold no regret.
May I live it all to Thy glory, Lord,

A day I don't want to forget.
May I henceforth a faithful servant be
And at the setting sun
Receive from Thy lips that greatest gift
Those wonderful words, "Well, done."

Frances E. Calkins

Each New Day Is Special!

Each new day is a special day to enjoy—
To watch the sun come up,
To hear the birds begin to sing,
To smell the newness of the day,
To hear the noises of life
awakening to the new dawn—
Makes each day a special day to enjoy.

Each new day is a special day to live—
To watch children playing in the sun,
To see the faces of loved ones,
To hear the voices of friends,
To be able to laugh and play,
To be able to work and love—
Makes each day a special day to live.

Noah S. Martin

Each day is a gift — I welcome it!
Life is a gift — I celebrate it!
God's love is a gift — I receive it!
Friendship is a gift — I embrace it!
Eternity is a gift — I await it!

Noah S. Martin

Lord of My Life, Lord of My Forevers...

I thank you that I have this day to live.
I thank you for being a part
  of all my yesterdays,
And I thank you that you hold my tomorrows
  in your hand.
Life is a gift—
  and I celebrate it!
The future is yours—
  and I welcome it!

B. J. Hoff

V

Appreciation for the New Day

Our Morning Star

His love greets us every morning
with new blessings for the day;
with each new sunrise, we embrace
the grace of God.
Ever mindful of his providence,
his never-failing care for us,
we celebrate the greatness
of our God.

B. J. Hoff

I Will Not Hurry Through This Day

I will not hurry through this day!
Lord, I will listen by the way,
To humming bees and singing birds,
To speaking trees and friendly words;
And for the moments in between
Steal glimpses of Thy great Unseen.

I will not hurry through this day;
I will take time to think and pray;
I will look up into the sky,
Where fleecy clouds and swallows fly;
And somewhere in the day, maybe
I will catch whispers, Lord, from Thee!

Ralph Spaulding Cushman

This Is a New Day

He's my fortress, my Protector,
My Everlasting Eternal Father,
Who will never leave me.
He is my True Love, my Very Life,
  My Comforter,
The healer of broken hearts and lives.

Because of the pit of pain I endured,
The place God and I walked through together,
I now see God in a new refreshing way.
My Father…He is very wise.
I see God anew in the freshness of the
  early morning light.
I thrill at the sound of crickets
  as they sing in harmony.

The most important, most precious things
  in life,
Are mostly near at hand—
Our families, children, spouses,
  parents and friends.
Why do we waste them so?
Why do we insist on employing our
  own wise plan?
Why do we need to go through valleys
To see who God really is?

Right outside our windows flowers
  are blooming.
The stars light the skies at night.
The crickets are singing.
The clouds hover and create darkness
  and then the refreshing rain,
And float away to allow the sun
  to shine again.

Surely the Lord is in this place.
Hope—He is—for our despair.
Faith—He is—for our doubts
Love—He is—for the deep need of it.
O, magnify the Lord!
Serve the Lord with gladness.
Sing unto the Lord a new song.
This is a New Day!

Delories (Dolly) Hostetler

Never a Day Goes By

Never a day goes by
But something new I see—
It may be a newborn flower
Or a bird on the tip of a tree.

Never a day goes by
But something new I hear—
It may be the call of a child
And her laughter sweet and clear.

Never a day goes by
But something new I touch—
It may be the hand of a friend
Of one I love so much.

Never a day goes by
But something new I know—
The blessing of strength restored
For the way God would have me go.

Author unknown

Treasure Each Moment

Treasure each moment of this day. Live it joyfully, expectantly, reverently, in deep appreciation for the gift of life this day offers. Don't put off living by waiting for a better day. Live each moment of this day to the best of your ability. The moments of each day make up the time of your life. Thus it is the sanctification of each moment that hallows your days and gives eternal meaning to your life. You are living for eternity in the moments of this day.

Noah S. Martin

VI

Praise for a New Day

This is the day which the Lord has made;
let us rejoice and be glad in it.
Psalm 118:24

Rejoice, O My Soul!

Rejoice, O my soul!
the night has gone,
the day has come.
The sun wraps itself
warmly about me.
I am awakened to new life.

A New Day! New Life!
Thank you, Lord, for its
    newness and freshness.
It will be a good day.
I sense your presence
    and know you are there.

Each new day
    causes me to believe in you.
You spoke —
    and the first day began.
You spoke again —
    and this day sprang forth.

Each new day is a miracle
    of your mighty power
    and your sure presence.
Surely your presence will
        hold me,
            keep me,
                guide me,
                    this day.
And your mighty power will
            recreate me —
                    each new day.

Noah S. Martin

Satisfy us in the morning with thy steadfast love,
that we may rejoice and be glad all our days.
Psalm 90:14

When Morning Gilds the Skies

When morning gilds the skies,
My heart awakening cries,
  "May Jesus Christ be praised!"
Alike at work and prayer,
On Thee I cast my care:
  "May Jesus Christ be praised!"

When sleep her balm denies,
My silent spirit cries,
  "May Jesus Christ be praised!"
The night becomes as day,
When from the heart we say,
  "May Jesus Christ be praised!"

From the German, c. 1800
Tr. by Edward Caswall

The steadfast love of the Lord never ceases,
his mercies never come to an end;
they are new every morning;
great is thy faithfulness.
Lamentations 3:22-23

Holy, holy, holy is the Lord of hosts;
the whole earth is full of his glory.
Isaiah 6:3

I will sing to the Lord
as long as I live;
I will sing praise to my God
while I have my being.
Psalm 104:33

My Morning Song

O Lord of life, Thy quickening voice awakes my morning song! In gladsome words I would rejoice that I to Thee belong. I see Thy light, I feel Thy wind; the world is Thy word;
Whatever wakes my heart and mind Thy presence is, My Lord.
Therefore I choose my highest part, and turn my face to Thee;
Therefore I stir my inmost heart to worship fervently.

George MacDonald

It is good to give thanks to the Lord,
to sing praises to the Most High;
to declare thy steadfast love in the morning,
and thy faithfulness by night.
Psalm 92:1-2

From the rising of the sun to its setting
the name of the Lord is to be praised!
Psalm 113:3

At Sunrise

Flowers rejoice when night is done,
Lift their heads to greet the sun;
Sweetest looks and odours raise,
In a silent hymn of praise.

So my heart would turn away
From the darkness to the day;
Lying open in God's sight
Like a flower in the light.

Henry Van Dyke

The heavens are telling the glory of God;
and the firmament proclaims his handiwork.
Day to day pours forth speech,
and night to night declares knowledge.
There is no speech, nor are there words;
their voice is not heard;
yet their voice goes out through all the earth,
and their words to the end of the world.
Psalm 19:1-4

Worthy art thou, our Lord and God,
to receive glory and honor and power,
for thou didst create all things,
and by thy will they existed and were created.
Revelation 4:11

Every day I will bless thee,
and praise thy name for ever and ever.
Great is the Lord, and greatly to be praised,
and his greatness is unsearchable.
Psalm 145:2-3

VII

The Presence of God

If You Meet God in the Morning, He'll Go with You Through the Day

"The earth is the Lord's
and the fullness thereof"—
It speaks of His greatness,
it sings of His love,
And each day at dawning
I lift my head high
And raise up my eyes
to the infinite sky...
I watch the night vanish
as a new day is born,
And I hear the birds sing
on the wings of the morn,

I see the dew glisten
in crystal-like splendor
While God, with a touch
that is gentle and tender,
Wraps up the night
and softly tucks it away
And hangs out the sun
to herald a new day…
And so I give thanks
and my heart kneels to pray—
"God, keep me and guide me
and go with me today."

Helen Steiner Rice

He is like the light of morning at sunrise.
2 Samuel 23:4, NIV

Whither shall I flee from thy Spirit?
Or whither shall I flee from thy presence?
If I ascend to heaven, thou art there!
If I make my bed in Sheol,
thou art there!
If I take the wings of the morning
and dwell in the uttermost parts of the sea,
even there thy hand shall lead me,
and thy right hand shall hold me.
Psalm 139:7-10

I Do Not Walk Alone

Because God walked with me
  Through all my yesteryears,
I now can read the meaning
    Of all my grief and tears.
Because God walks with me
  Within this world today,
I face tough times assured
    He'll help me all the way.
Because God walks with me
  Down paths untrod, unknown,
I know no fear because
    I do not walk alone.

Perry Tanksley

Lo, I am with you always,
to the close of the age.

the Lord Jesus Christ
(Matthew 28:20)

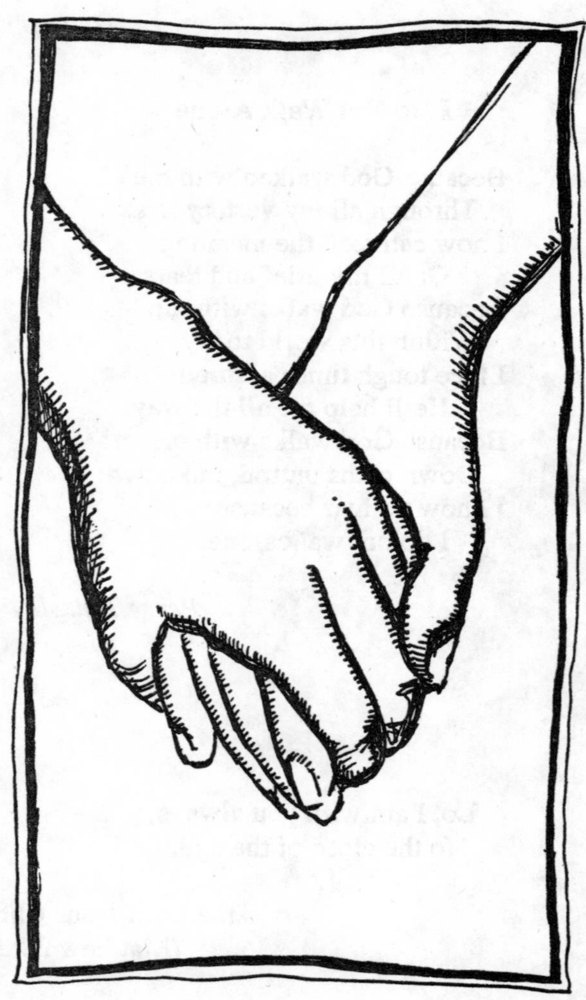

VIII

Morning Prayers

Good Morning, God!

You are ushering in another day
Untouched and freshly new
So here I am to ask You, God,
If you'll renew me, too.
Forgive the many errors
That I made yesterday
And let me try again, dear God,
To walk closer in **THY WAY...**
But, Father, I am well aware
I can't make it on my own
So **TAKE MY HAND AND HOLD IT TIGHT**
For I can't **WALK ALONE!**

Helen Steiner Rice

I, O Lord, cry to thee;
in the morning my prayer comes before thee.
Psalm 88:13

My voice shalt thou hear in the morning,
O Lord; in the morning will I direct
my prayer unto thee, and will look up.
Psalm 5:3, KJV

Prayer

Ere thou risest from thy bed,
Speak to God whose wings were spread
O'er thee in the helpless night:
Lo, He wakes thee now with light!
Lift thy burden and thy care
In the mighty arms of prayer.

Lord, the newness of this day
Calls me to an untried way:
Let me gladly take the road,
Give me strength to bear my load,
Thou my guide and helper be—
I will travel through with Thee.

Henry Van Dyke

Every day I call upon thee, O Lord;
I spread out my hands to thee.
Psalm 88:9

A Morning Prayer

Lord, in the quiet of this morning hour,
Let me feel thy love and power.
Let me so full of thy Spirit be,
That others can see the Christ in me.
Let me reflect thy presence sweet
To everyone I chance to meet.
Let me a friend to people be
That they, too, will search for Thee.
Let me add to this, thy day,
Love and peace in every way.

Estells Wright Scegedin

Prayer at Dawn

When morning breaks and I face the day,
This, dear Lord, is what I pray.
That when the same day fades to gray,
Some child of yours may happier be,
May find himself more close to Thee,
Because I lived this day.

Jule Creaser

Day by Day

Day by day, Dear Lord,
Of Thee three things I pray:
To see Thee more clearly,
Love Thee more dearly,
Follow Thee more nearly,
Day by Day.

St. Richard of Chichester

In the Quiet of the Morning

In the quiet of the morning,
Oh, how sweet it is to come
Just to talk a bit with Jesus
Ere the crowding duties come.

Just to kneel there for a moment
With your head upon His breast,
All your problems laid before Him,
Every human need confessed.

Oh, the loving strength that surges
From His heart to yours all day;
Like a bright and shining armor,
Just because you knelt to pray!

Alice H. Mortensen

Jesus, My Ever-Present Pilot and Guide...

Help me to begin each new day
with your name in my thoughts,
your love in my heart,
your Spirit at my side
to guide and lead me.
Help me, Lord, to celebrate in the quiet
the splendor of another sunrise,
to bow in thanksgiving
before the incredible beauty
of a clear blue sky,
and to stand in awe
as I add my voice of praise
to nature's chorus.
Every morning, Lord,
every precious day...
I will sing *Alleluia.*

B. J. Hoff

Children's Morning Prayers

Good morning, God! I am so glad that you are my friend. Together we make a great team. I am not afraid of anything when you are beside me. It will be a good day if you will think through my brain, talk through my tongue, and smile at people through my face. In my work or play, may my friends and even strangers see that I love you.
Amen!

Robert Schuller

Good morning, God! Thank you for your beautiful world! I want to make your world even more beautiful. So may my face be like happy sunshine and not a dark cloud.
Amen.

Robert Schuller

I rise before dawn and cry for help;
I hope in thy words.
My eyes are awake before the
watches of the night,
that I may meditate upon thy promise.
Psalm 119:147-148

IX

The Meaning of the Day

All the flowers of all the tomorrows
are in the seeds of today.

from *Apples of Gold*

I have no Yesterdays
Time took them away;
Tomorrow may not be—
But I have Today.

Pearl Yeadon McGinnis

Choose this day whom you will serve.
Joshua 24:15

Let every day
be a dream
we can touch.

Let every day
be a love
we can feel.

Let every day
be a reason
to live.

Claudia Adrienne Grandi

A Day Is Born

Lo, here hath been dawning another blue day;
Think, wilt thou let it slip useless away?

Out of eternity this new day is born,
Into eternity at night it will return.

Behold it aforetime no eye ever did;
So soon it forever from all eyes hid.

Here hath been dawning another blue day;
Think, wilt thou let it slip useless away?

Thomas Caryle

Thank You, O God, For the Opportunities of This Day

Thank you, O God, for the opportunities of this day.
Give me the mind of Christ;
Keep me filled with the Holy Spirit.
Give me a heart of love
  that I will seize each opportunity
  as a moment to serve you.

I will need courage to be truthful,
  honest and open;
I will need wisdom and strength
  for the day.
I will need your light
  to show me the way.

And, yes, O God,
  how about some joy!
I want my days to praise you,
  my life to bless you!
Put a smile on my face,
  A song in my heart,
  A sparkle in my eyes,
  A spring in my step.

There's no greater honor, O God,
  than to be your child
  and to walk with you through the day.
And when evening comes,
  may I rest in peace,
  knowing that I have walked with you today.

Noah S. Martin

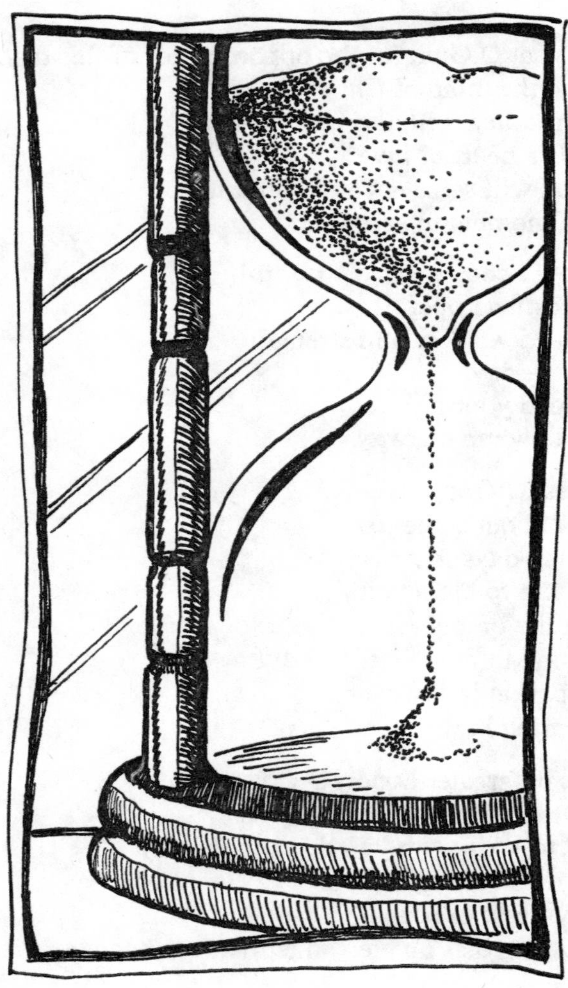

Richer Today

You are richer today than you were yesterday...
if you have laughed often, given something,
forgiven even more, made a new friend today,
or made a stepping-stone of stumbling-blocks;
if you have thought more of "thyself" than of "myself,"
or if you have succeeded in being
cheerful even if you were weary. You are richer
tonight than you were this morning...if you have taken
time to trace the handiwork of God in
the commonplace things of life, or if you have
learned to count out things that really do not
count, or if you have been a little blinder to
the faults of friend or foe. You are richer if
a little child has smiled at you, and a stray
dog has licked your hand, or if you have looked
for the best in others, and have given others
the best in you.

author unknown

This is the beginning
of a new day.
God has given me this day
to use it as I will.
I can waste it
or grow in its light
and be of service to others.
But what I do
with this day is important
because I have exchanged
a day of my life for it.
When tomorrow comes,
today will be gone forever.
I hope I will not regret
the price I paid for it.

author unknown

Here, Lord, is my life.
I place it on the altar today.
Use it as you will.

Albert Schweitzer

So teach us to number our days
that we may get a heart of wisdom.
Psalm 90:12

To confront each day
with hope shining in your eyes,
to welcome the day
with reverence for the opportunities
it contains,
to greet everyone you meet
with laughter and love,
to be gentle, kind, and courteous
toward friend and foe, and
to enjoy the satisfaction of work well done
during precious hours that will never return—
that is the way to leave your footprints.

Og Mandino

Take the Time To Do the Things That Will Bring You Joy

Your life can be happier
If you wake up each morning and give thanks
for having another day to reach
  towards your dreams.
If you share some kind words with your
family and friends,
and listen to what they say to you.
If you spend a moment while you're working
to forgive yourself for any mistakes you
  may have made,
and to forgive those who may have hurt you.
If you keep your thoughts on the things
  you value in life,
and don't worry about what is not important.
If you try to accomplish something
  you've never done before,
because you'll be challenging yourself to grow,
as well as making your life more interesting.
If you do something to make someone happy,
for that person's joy will make you happy.
If you are as true to yourself as you can be,
for your honesty will bring you peace of mind.
If, when you lay your head down to
  sleep at night,
you give thanks once more for the opportunities

you had during the day to achieve and to love.
You can be a happier you
if you take the time to do the things
that will bring you joy.

Donna Levine

A Day Worthwhile

I count that day as wisely spent
In which I do some good
For someone who is far away
Or shares my neighborhood.
A day devoted to the deed
that lends a helping hand
And demonstrates a willingness
To care and understand.
I long to be of usefulness
In little ways and large
Without a selfish motive
And without the slightest charge.
Because in my philosophy
There never is a doubt
That all of us here on earth
Must help each other out.
I feel that day is fruitful
And the time is worth the while
When I promote the happiness
Of one enduring smile.

author unknown

You are the light of the world.
the Lord Jesus Christ
(Matthew 5:14)

The hero is one who kindles a great light in the world, who sets up blazing torches in the dark streets of life for men to see by. The saint is one who walks through the dark paths of the world, himself a light.

Felix Adler

Lamplighter

He has taken his bright candle and is gone
Into another room I cannot find,
But anyone can tell where he has been
By all the little lights he leaves behind.

anonymous

A Prayer for the Day

I don't want to go through life, O God, just living out my days. I want something to live for, something to do that has meaning, and something to say that will make a difference in this world. Life is too precious to waste it; the days are too short to fritter away.

O, speak to my heart, Lord, that I may know the meaning of my days. Lead me aright, that I may find the purpose for my life. Guide my days, that I may fulfill Your plan for their time.

May my days praise You, my life glorify You, and my time on earth have meaning for eternity. So that at the dawning of the New Day, I may be present to praise Your name for ever and ever. Amen.

Noah S. Martin

For a Day of My Life

This is the beginning of a new day. God has given this day to me to use as I will. I can waste it or use it. I can make it a day long to be remembered for its joy, its beauty and its achievement, or it can be filled with pettiness.

When night comes, I want to look back without regret, and forward with radiant spirit and thankful heart.

Samuel F. Pugh

We must work the works of him who sent me, while it is day; night comes, when no one can work.

the Lord Jesus Christ
(John 9:4)

X

Courage for Each New Day

Blessed be the Lord,
who daily bears us up;
God is our salvation.

Psalm 68:19

Be strong and of good courage;
be not frightened,
neither be dismayed;
for the Lord your God is with you
wherever you go.

Joshua 1:9

New Day

God turns each morning a new page for me and says,
"See here, my child, a new-born day, glorious and shining,
Take it and use it well.

Put far behind thee yesterday's dark thoughts,
Its failures, its vain stumblings, and its griefs.

The robin's song rings a bright bugle call
to rouse the slumbering heart.

Arise my child and set thee forth
with dauntless courage still.

One day may change the face of all the world.

One day, lived fearlessly, thy hand in mine,
Shall conquer all things and make all things thine.

One day — one glorious day!

Arise my child!

Fear nothing for I am with thee today."

Grace Bush

He gives power to the faint,
and to him who has no might
he increases strength.

Isaiah 40:29

Always Remember the Strength Within You

Tomorrow might seem
as if it will never come
when your difficulties
continue to absorb
all of your efforts.
But there is hope
that a better tomorrow is near;
there is strength within you
that will help you bear
all the burdens of today.

jodi mae

The Lord is my strength and my shield;
in him my heart trusts;
so I am helped and my heart exults,
and with my song I give thanks to him.

Psalm 28:7

Call upon me in the day of trouble;
and I will deliver you,
and you shall glorify me.
Psalm 50:15

He Cares

I know that I can trust the Lord
To keep the stars in place,
To grant the lark, the rose, the oak
His wisdom and His grace.

I know that I can trust the Lord
To send the morning light,
To turn each winter into spring,
To rule each depth, each height.

Then why should I refuse to trust
Those things I cannot see
To Him who knows tomorrow's needs?
He cares for you and me.

Phyllis C. Michael

I will sing aloud of thy steadfast
love in the morning.
For thou hast been to me a fortress
and a refuge in the day of my distress.
Psalm 59:16

Courage for This Day

Give me courage for this day, O Lord.
Some days I need to stand up
  for what I believe;
I need to speak the truth;
I need to turn and run from evil.
Other days I need to stand and deal
  with evil face-to-face.
The battle can be tough and wearisome.

Some days put me to the test.
My back is against the wall.
My heart throbs and my knees grow
  weak and trembling.
My faith wants to break up and crack
  under the strain.

In these days, O God, I look to you
  for help and courage.
Be —
  my steady hand,
  my sure legs,
  my sound mind,
  my quiet heart,
  my firm trust in you.

Then I shall learn —
  to praise you through the storm,
  to sing through the night,
  to trust you in the dark,
  to honor you in the turmoil,
  to serve you in the conflict,
  to know your love in my heart.

Noah S. Martin

Build a little fence of trust around today;
Fill the space with loving deeds and therein stay;
Look not through the sheltering bars upon tomorrow;
God will help thee bear what comes of joy or sorrow.

Mary Francis Butt

Wait for the Lord;
be strong, and let your heart
take courage;
yea, wait for the Lord!

Psalm 27:14

What God Hath Promised

God hath not promised skies always blue,
Flower-strewn pathways all our lives through;
God hath not promised sun without rain,
Joy without sorrow, peace without pain.

But God hath promised strength for the day,
Rest for the labor, light for the way,
Grace for the trials, help from above,
Unfailing sympathy, undying love.

Annie Johnson Flint

The eternal God is your dwelling place,
and underneath are the everlasting arms.
Deuteronomy 33:27

This, Too, Will Pass Away

If I can endure for this minute
Whatever is happening to me,
No matter how heavy my heart is
Or how "dark" the moment may be—
If I can but keep on believing
What I know in my heart is true,
That "darkness will fade with the morning"
And that THIS WILL PASS AWAY, TOO—
Then nothing can ever disturb me
Or fill me with fear,
For as sure as NIGHT BRINGS THE DAWNING
"MY MORNING" is bound to appear.

Helen Steiner Rice

Weeping may tarry for the night,
but joy comes with the morning.
Psalm 30:5

When the righteous cry for help, the Lord hears,
and delivers them out of all their troubles.

The Lord is near to the brokenhearted,
and saves the crushed in spirit.

Many are the afflictions of the righteous;
but the Lord delivers him out of them all.
Psalm 34:17-19

Hope for the Dark Days

The sun does not always shine
everyday for everyone.
Some days are awakened
to cold, wintry storms.
Illness, death, disappointments,
broken dreams,
A deep aching of the soul
comes our way
To make some days long and hard.

Our Lord suffered one day, too.
He was afflicted and beaten,
like a sheep led to the slaughter.
He cried out in the darkness —
"Let this cup pass from me!"
But He was led on to suffer,
to bleed, to die.

In the end He cried,
  "Father, into thy hands
  I commit my spirit!"
And then He died.

Then He arose!

Now He is seated at the right hand
  of the Father in power and glory.

In our days of suffering,
  light is turned into darkness,
  joy gives way to sorrow,
  peace succumbs to disarray,
  hope is dashed by despair,
And all is dark — so dark.

But in the end —
  the new day will break forth!
  the sun will shine through the darkness!
  evil will forever be conquered!
  sorrow and sighing will be no more!
  new life will rise up to be forever!
  Christ will come to reign in light and peace!

And, in the new day,
  all will be
  Light and Love,
  Joy and Peace.

Even so, come quickly, Lord Jesus!

Noah S. Martin

XI

One Day at a Time

Give us this day our daily bread.
the Lord Jesus Christ
(Matthew 6:11)

Do Not Worry

It has well been said that no man ever sank under the burden of the day. It is when tomorrow's burden is added to the burden of today that the weight is more than a man can bear. Never load yourself so, my friends. If you find yourself so loaded, at least remember this: it is your own doing, not God's. He begs you to leave the future to Him, and mind the present.

George MacDonald

One day at a time—
this is enough.
Do not look back
and grieve over the past,
for it is gone;
and do not be troubled
about the future,
for it has not yet come.
Live in the present,
and make it so beautiful
that it will be worth
remembering.

Ida Scott Taylor

Therefore do not be anxious about tomorrow,
for tomorrow will be anxious for itself.
Let the day's own trouble be sufficient
for the day.

the Lord Jesus Christ
(Matthew 6:34)

Leave tomorrow's trouble to tomorrow's strength; tomorrow's work to tomorrow's time; tomorrow's trial to tomorrow's grace and to tomorrow's God.

anonymous

Do not be troubled, O my soul, about tomorrow. The best assurance for tomorrow is to walk with God today. You will then wake up each morning in the comfort of the presence of God. The future is not yours to see or know. Leave it in the hands of the One who sees and knows all things. In His love and care for you He will lead you day by day and step by step until one day the last step will be taken into the glorious New Day of life eternal.

Noah S. Martin

By day the Lord commands his steadfast love;
and at night his song is with me,
a prayer to the God of my life.
Psalm 42:8

I have four things to learn in life:
to think clearly, without hurry
or confusion;
to love everybody sincerely;
to act in everything with the
highest motives;
to trust in God unhesitatingly.

Helen Keller

Walk with Me Today

Lord, I often think of the past,
what was done,
what was left undone;
the decisions I made that I cannot change,
the seeds that were sown that cannot be reclaimed.

I often wonder, how would things be different
if I had prayed more often,
spoken more kindly,
read your Word more faithfully,
sought after your heart more diligently.
I bow my head in deep humility.

I often worry about the future, too—
what will happen to me,
to the ones I love and care for,
to the world, the economy, my job.
How long can I make it in this world? I ask.
With all its problems, how long can this world go on?

Then you spoke to my heart and said,
"I know you; I love you;
You are my child.
Hold on to me.
Trust me.
I have brought you to this moment.
My faithfulness has led you to this day.

Your past is forgiven,
Your tomorrow is in my care.
I, who have brought you this far,
will never leave you or forsake you.
Come, walk with me—today.
I will take care of you tomorrow."

Noah S. Martin

Cast all your anxieties on him,
for he cares about you.

I Peter 5:7

Anyone can carry his or her burden, however hard, until nightfall. Anyone can do his work, however hard, for one day. Anyone can live sweetly, patiently, lovingly, purely, till the sun goes down. And this is all that life really means.

Robert Louis Stevenson

One Day at a Time

One day at a time, with its
failures and fears,
With its hurts and mistakes,
with its weakness and tears,
with its portion of pain and
its burden of care;
One day at a time we must meet
and must bear.
One day at a time—but the day
is so long.

And the heart is not brave, and
the soul is not strong.
O thou pitiful Christ, be Thou
near all the way:
Give courage and patience and
strength for the day.

Swift cometh the answer, so
clear and so sweet;
"Yea, I will be with thee, nor
fail thee, nor grieve;
I will not forsake thee; I will
never leave."

One day at a time, and the day
is His day;
He hath numbered its hours,
though they haste or delay;

His grace is sufficient,
    we walk not alone;
As the day, so the strength
    that He giveth His own.

Annie Johnson Flint

Live One Day at a Time

We cannot change the past;
we just need to keep
the good memories
and acquire wisdom
from the mistakes we've made.
We cannot predict the future;
we just need to hope and pray
for the best and what is right,
and believe that's how it will be.
We can live one day at a time,
enjoying the present
and always seeking to become
a more loving and better person.

Karen Berry

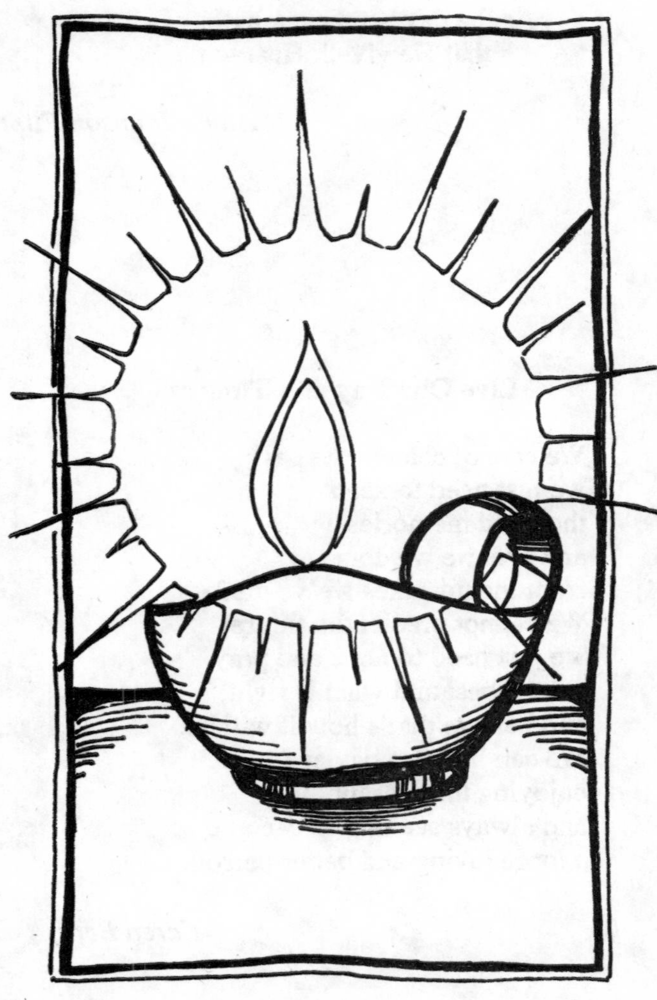

Day by Day

Charge not thyself with the weight of a year,
Child of the Master, faithful and dear:
Choose not the cross for the coming week,
For that is more than He bids thee seek.

Bend not thine arms for tomorrow's load;
Thou mayest leave that to thy precious God.
"Daily," only He saith to thee,
"Take up thy cross and follow Me."

author unknown

Look to This Day

Look to this day, for it is life. The very life of life. In its brief course lies all the realities and verities of existence, the bliss of growth, the splendor of action, the glory of power—for yesterday is but a dream and tomorrow is only a vision. But today, well lived, makes every yesterday a dream of happiness and every tomorrow a vision of hope. Look well, therefore, to this day.

From the Sanscrit

Day by Day

Day by day, and with each passing moment,
Strength I find to meet my trials here.
Trusting in my Father's wise bestowment,
I've no cause for worry or for fear.
He whose heart is kind beyond all measure
Gives unto each day what He deems best,
Lovingly its part of pain and pleasure,
Mingling toil with peace and rest.

Every day the Lord himself is near me,
With a special mercy for each hour.
All my care He fain would bear and cheer me,
He whose name is Counselor and Power.
The protection of His child and treasure
Is a charge that on himself He laid;
"As thy days, thy strength shall be in measure,"
This the pledge to me He made.

Help me then in every tribulation
So to trust Thy promises, O Lord,
That I lose not faith's sweet consolation,
Offered me within Thy holy Word.
Help me, Lord, when toil and trouble meeting,
E'er to take, as from a Father's hand,
One by one, the days, the moments fleeting,
Till I reach the promised land.

Lina Sandell

Be patient to live one day at a time
as Jesus taught us, letting yesterday
go and leaving tomorrow until it arrives.

from *Apples of Gold*

All I have seen teaches me to trust the
Creator for all that I have not seen.

Ralph Waldo Emerson

As your days, so shall your strength be.
Deuteronomy 33:25

XII

Guidance for Each New Day

Lead me, O God, in thy righteousness...
make thy way straight before me.

Psalm 5:8

The Way

Not for one single day
Can I discern my way,
But this I surely know—
Who gives the day,
Will show the way,
So I securely go.

John Oxenham

Tomorrow's Way

I know not if tomorrow's way
  Be steep or rough;
But when His hand is guiding me,
  That is enough.
And so, although the veil has hid
  tomorrow's way,
I walk with perfect faith and trust,
  Through each today.

The love of God has hung a veil
  Around tomorrow.
That we may not its beauty see
  Nor trouble borrow.
But, oh, 'tis sweeter far, to trust
  His unseen hand,
And know that all the paths of life,
  His wisdom planned.

author unknown

Let me hear in the morning of thy steadfast love,
for in thee I put my trust.
Teach me the way I should go,
for to thee I lift up my soul.

Psalm 143:8

Thy word is a lamp to my feet
and a light to my path.
Psalm 119:105

Make me to know thy ways, O Lord;
teach me thy paths.
Lead me in thy truth, and teach me,
for thou art the God of my salvation;
for thee I wait all the day long.
Psalm 25:4-5

The Lord is God,
and he has given us light.
Psalm 118:27

Yea, thou art my lamp, O Lord,
and my God lightens my darkness.
II Samuel 22:29

Oh send out thy light and thy truth;
let them lead me,
let them bring me to thy holy hill
and to thy dwelling!
Psalm 43:3

Thank You for Your Love

O God, lead me through each new day,
I cannot see my way.
Often I stumble and complain
    that the day is long,
        the road is hard,
And I feel scared and alone.

I marvel at your grace that lets
    me start over each new day.
You could give up on me.
But each new day you—
    wake me with the dawn,
    breathe into me the breath of life,
    get me up on my feet,
    and hold me close to your heart,
        and you whisper,
            "I love you."

Thank you for your love, dear God.
I can go through each day
    if I know you love me.
Forgive me for the times
    I have not loved you.
Your love surrounds me,
Your grace forgives me,
Your care enfolds me,
Your light guides me,
Your power recreates me,
Your presence comforts me.
I walk close beside you,
    and I whisper,
        "I love you, Lord."

Noah S. Martin

O give thanks to the Lord, for he is good;
his steadfast love endures for ever!
Psalm 118:1

I have loved you with an everlasting love;
therefore I have continued my faithfulness to you.
Jeremiah 31:3

I love the Lord, because he has heard
my voice and my supplications.
Psalm 116:1

XIII

Beginning Anew

Bring Tomorrow's Dawning

If I have failed to do a thoughtful deed,
Or turned my back on anyone in need,
If I've ignored the clouds in someone's skies,
Or missed the chance to wipe another's eyes,
If I have spoken words of bitterness,
If I have failed or faltered, more or less,
If I've forgotten the golden rule someway—
Lord, bring tomorrow's dawning, so I may
Make up for all I've left undone today!

Alice Joyce Davidson

This Day of New Beginnings

Each new day causes me to believe in you.
You spoke — and the first day began.
You spoke again — and this day sprang forth.
Speak now — so I can spring forth as the new day.
As surely as this day brings forth new life,
So can I begin anew and bring forth new life.
Your creative power touches me and heals me.
  I move from darkness to light,
  From slumber to life,
  From sin to grace,
  From fear to rest,
And I experience my new day.

Oh, thank you, Lord, for this moment of grace —
  this day of new beginnings!
This is the day that you have made;
I will be glad and rejoice in it!

Noah S. Martin

It Took a Miracle

It took a miracle to put
  the stars in place.
It took a miracle to hang
  the world in space;
But when He saved my soul,
Cleansed and made me whole,
It took a miracle of
  love and grace!

John W. Peterson

Therefore, if anyone is in Christ,
he is a new creation;
the old has passed away, behold,
the new has come.

2 Corinthians 5:17

A New Day

Finish every day and be done with it. You have done what you could. Some blunders and absurdities no doubt crept in; forget them as soon as you can. Tomorrow is a new day; begin it well and serenely and with too high a spirit to be cumbered with your old nonsense. This day is all that is good and fair. It is too dear, with its hopes and invitations, to waste a moment on the yesterdays.

Ralph Waldo Emerson

Starting afresh patiently and in good cheer and hope is the mark of the Christian. One of the helpful definitions of Christianity is this: the Christian life is a series of new beginnings.

John B. Coburn

Every day is a birthday,
for every day we are
born anew.

Ellen Browning Scripps

A New Day! A New Life!

Each day at dawning we have but to pray
That all the mistakes that we made yesterday
Will be blotted out and forgiven by grace,
For God in His love will completely efface
All that is past and He'll grant a new start
To all who are truly repentant at heart—
And well may man pause in awesome-like wonder
That our Father in heaven who dwells far asunder
Could still remain willing to freely forgive
The shabby, small lives we so selfishly live
And still would be mindful of sin-ridden man
Who constantly goes on defying God's plan—
But this is the gift of God's limitless love
A gift that we all are so unworthy of,
But God gave it to us and all we need do
Is to ask God's forgiveness and begin life anew.

Helen Steiner Rice

Sing to the Lord, bless his name;
tell of his salvation from day to day.
Psalm 96:2

Do not marvel that I say to you,
"You must be born anew."
the Lord Jesus Christ
(John 3:7)

How often we wish for another chance
to make a fresh beginning,
A chance to blot out our mistakes
and change failure into winning—
And it does not take a special time
to make a brand new start,
It only takes the deep desire
to try with all our heart
To live a little better
and to always be forgiving
And to add a little sunshine
to the world in which we're living—
So never give up in despair
and think that you are through
For there's always a tomorrow
and a chance to start anew.

Helen Steiner Rice

Each new day is an opportunity to start all over again...to cleanse our minds and hearts anew and to clarify our vision. And let us not clutter up today with the leavings of other days.

from *Apples of Gold*

The same God who created the day for you,
can recreate you for the day.

Noah S. Martin

Every day is a fresh beginning;
Listen, my soul, to the glad refrain,
And, in spite of old sorrow...
and possibly pain,
Take heart with the day, and begin again.

Susan Coolidge

XIV

Eternal Day

Each Step I Take

Each step I take my Saviour goes before me,
And with His loving hand He leads the way.
And with each breath I whisper, "I adore Thee";
Oh, what joy to walk with Him each day.

Each step I take, I know that He will guide me;
To higher ground He ever leads me on;
Until some day the last step will be taken,
Each step I take just leads me closer home.

W. Elmo Mercer

Death is not extinguishing the light;
it is putting out the lamp because dawn has come.

from *Apples of Gold*

Dawn

Dawn is such a wonderful time, O Lord,
One moment it is dark, still night;
then the next moment there is light,
not a lot of light at first, just a glimmer
that begins to glow, letting the world know
that it isn't quite night anymore.
Day is on the way...and then...
the day is here!

I'm glad to wake up every day and see
that it really is a new day, another gift from You
for me to live in and enjoy.
Thank You for the day, O Lord, for each new dawn,
for each reminder, every day, that You are there
as You were that lovely Easter day
to greet the dawn, alive,
and let the world know
that something new was happening,
the dawn of another—an eternal Day!

author unknown

The path of the righteous is like the light of dawn,
which shines brighter and brighter until full day.
Proverbs 4:18

And I saw no temple in the city,
for its temple is the Lord God
the Almighty and the Lamb.
And the city has no need of sun or moon
to shine upon it,
for the glory of the Lord is its light,
and its lamp is the Lamb...
and its gates shall never be shut by day—
and there shall be no night there.
Revelation 21:22-25

Some Golden Daybreak

Some golden daybreak, Jesus will come;
Some golden daybreak, battles all won;
He'll shout the victory, break through the blue;
Some golden daybreak, for me, for you.

C. A. Blackmore

A New Day

In the freshness of the morning
When the darkness fades from dawn,
And the birds announce the coming
Of a new day, with a joyful song—
Awakened, I am reminded
Of my Father's vigilant care,
And in prayerful adoration
I ponder in His presence there.
Another day is yet to come,
When darkness shall ever be past—
And night will flee and be no more,
When Christ shall come and reign at last.
That glorious day shall never end—
Earth's trials and woes will pass away,
And in God's home we shall ever live
Where there will be an everlasting day.

Mrs. Harmon Eggleston

Our Creator would never have made
such lovely days,
and given us the deep hearts
to enjoy them,
above and beyond all thought,
unless we were meant to be immortal.

Nathaniel Hawthorne

When I awake, I am still with thee.
Psalm 139:18

Still, Still with Thee

Still, still with Thee,
when purple morning breaketh,
When the bird waketh,
and the shadows flee;
Fairer than morning,
lovelier than the daylight,
Dawns the sweet consciousness,
I am with Thee.

Alone with Thee, amid the
mystic shadows,
The solemn hush of nature
newly born;
Alone with thee in
breathless adoration,
In the calm dew and freshness
of the morn.

Still, still with Thee! As to
each new born morning
A fresh and solemn splendor
still is given,
So does this blessed consciousness,
awakening,
Each day brings nearness unto Thee
and heaven.

Each day brings nearness unto Thee
  and heaven.

So shall it be at last, in that
  bright morning,
When the soul waketh and life's
  shadow's flee;
O in that hour, fairer than
  daylight dawning,
Shall rise the glorious thought,
  "I am with Thee."

Harriet Beecher Stowe

Until Then

My heart can sing when I pause to remember
A heartache here is but a stepping stone
Along a trail that's winding always upward —
This troubled world is not my final home.

But until then my heart will go on singing.
Until then with joy I'll carry on —
Until the day my eyes behold the city,
Until the day God calls me home.

Stuart Hamblen

"Behold, I make all things new."
the Lord Jesus Christ
(Revelation 21:5)

Bright New World

Someday a bright new wave will break
upon the shore,
And there will be no sickness,
no more crying,
no more war;
And little children never will go
hungry anymore.
And there'll be a bright new morning
over there.
There'll be a bright new world
for us to share.

Someday there'll be an end to unkind
words and cruel.
The man who said, there is no God,
will know he is a fool;
And peace will be a way of life
with love the only rule.
And there'll be a bright new morning
over there.
There'll be a bright new world
for us to share.

Someday we know not when,
when time on earth is done,
And those redeemed from every land
will all become as one
With voices of all ages praising God
the three in one.

And there'll be a bright new morning
  over there.
There'll be a bright new world
  for us to share.

Flo Price

And night shall be no more;
they need no light of lamp or sun,
for the Lord God will be their light,
and they shall reign for ever and ever.
Revelation 22:5

For I am sure that neither death, nor life,
nor angels, nor principalities, nor things
present, nor things to come, nor powers,
nor height, nor depth, nor anything else in
all creation, will be able to separate us
from the love of God in Christ Jesus our Lord.
Romans 8:38-39

Benediction

When the last sunrise on this earth has come,
When the last day has gone beneath the clouds,
When the last bird has sung its morning watch,
When the last flowers of spring no longer bloom,
When the last fragrance after the rain is gone,
When the last "Good Morning" has been said,
When the last day on earth has ended
and the morning breaks no more—

Then may you awaken to the joy of a New Day
in which the sun never rises or sets,
for all is light;
in which the day is filled with song and praise,
for all is joy;
in which flowers bloom eternally,
for all is beautiful;
in which friendships endure forever,
for all is love;
in which sorrow and sighing shall be no more,
for all is peace;
in which night does not come,
for Christ is the Light;
in which time never ends,
for all is eternal.

Into His blessings which are forever,
Into His care which is keeping,
Into His joy which is complete,
Into His love which is unending,
Into His day which is eternal,
You are set free to fulfill the purpose
of your days on earth:

Surely goodness and mercy shall follow me
all the days of my life;
and I shall dwell in the house of
the Lord for ever.

Psalm 23:6

Amen!

Noah S. Martin

Acknowledgments

Every effort has been made to identify, locate, contact and secure the permission of publishers and/or authors to use copyrighted material contained in this book. Unfortunately, a number of selections could not be traced to a particular original publishing source, such as a poem found on the wall of the Cambria County Detention Center, an embroidered one that hangs on the wall of New Day's office in Johnstown, and another one that arrived in the mail. Any inadvertent omission of credit will be gladly corrected in future editions.

Grateful acknowledgment is hereby expressed to the following who have granted permission to include copyrighted materials in this book.

Credit Lines

Unless otherwise noted, all scripture taken from the Revised Standard Version © 1946, 1952, 1971 by Division of Christian Education of the National Council of the Churches of Christ in the United States of America.

B. J. Hoff's poems from *Thorns and Thrones*, by B. J. Hoff. © 1991, Warner Press, Inc. (Anderson, IN). Used by permission.

Words to *Morning Has Broken* reprinted by permission of Harold Ober Associates Incorporated. © 1957 by Eleanor Farjeon.

Words to *Each Step I Take* by Elmo Mercer © 1953 Singspiration Music/ASCAP. All Rights Reserved. Used by permission of Benson Music Group, Inc.

Quotes by Albert Schweitzer and John B. Coburn from *Great Quotes & Illustrations*, George Sweeting, 1985, Word, Inc., Dallas, TX. Used with permission.

Excerpts by Jo Petty on pages 53, 91, 105, 109 from *Apples of Gold* © 1962 Jo Petty, renewed 1990. Published by the C.R. Gibson Company, Norwalk, CT 06856. All rights reserved.

Helen Steiner Rice's poetry used with permission of The Helen Steiner Rice Foundation, Suite 2100, Atrium Two, 221 East Fourth Street, Cincinnati, OH 45202.

Ralph Spaulding Cushman's poems "I Will Not Hurry" and "The Secret" used by permission of Dr. Robert E. Cushman.

Excerpt from "The Sanscrit" from *Better Than Medicine: A Merry Heart* by Leroy Brownlow, Brownlow Publishing Co., Inc., © 1967. Used with permission.

Poem "I Do Not Walk Alone" by Perry Tanksley. © 1980 by Perry Tanksley. Used by permission.

Poetry by Helen Keller has been reprinted with permission from the American Foundation for the Blind, 15 West 16th Street, New York, NY 10011.

Excerpt from "Renascence" by Edna St. Vincent Millay. © 1917, 1945 by Edna St. Vincent Millay.

"He Cares" © 1969 by Phyllis C. Michael in *Beside Still Waters*. Used by permission of the author.

"Bring Tomorrow's Dawning" from the book *Because I Love You* by Alice Joyce Davidson, © 1982 by Alice Joyce Davidson. Used by permission of Baker Book House.

"It Took A Miracle" © 1948, renewed 1976 by John W. Peterson Music Company. All rights reserved. Used by permission.

"Prayer at Dawn" by Jule Creaser reprinted with permission from Guideposts Magazine. © 1969 by Guideposts Associates, Inc., Carmel, NY 10512.

"Bright New World" by Flo Price © 1969 by Bud John Songs, Inc., 2505 21st Ave. South, Nashville, TN 37212. All Rights Reserved. Used by permission.

"Live One Day at a Time" by Karen Berry © 1990 by Blue Mountain Arts, Inc., All rights reserved. Reprinted by permission of Blue Mountain Arts.

Henry Van Dyke's poem "Matins" appears as "At Sunrise" and "New Day" ("Three Prayers for Sleeping and Waking",

III) appears as "New Day". Reprinted with permission of Charles Scribner's Sons, an imprint of Macmillan Publishing Company, from *The Poems of Henry Van Dyke* (NY: Charles Scribner's Sons, 1920).

Some Golden Daybreak by C. A. Blackmore and Carl Blackmore © 1934, renewed 1962 by The Rodeheaver Co. (a div. of WORD, INC.). All Rights Reserved. Used by Permission.

Excerpt by Og Mandino taken from *A Better Way To Live* by Og Mandino, © 1990 by Bantam Books, Inc. Used by permission.

"Children's Morning Prayers" by Robert Schuller from *Positive Prayers for Power-Filled Living* by Robert H. Schuller. © 1976 by Robert H. Schuller. Used by permission of the publisher, Dutton, an imprint of New American Library, a division of Penguin Books USA Inc.

"For A Day Of My Life" by Dr. Samuel F. Pugh. © 1958 by Dr. Samuel F. Pugh. Used by permission of the author.

Poem "Take The Time To Do The Things That Will Bring You Joy" by Donna Levine © 1987. Used by permission of the author.

Quote by Beverley Nichols from *The Fool Hath Said* by Beverley Nichols. © 1935, 1936 by Beverley Nichols. Used by permission of Doubleday Publishing Company.

"Until Then" by Stuart Hamblen © 1958 Hamblen Music Co. International Copyright Secured. All rights reserved.

Poem "In the Quiet of the Morning" by Alice H. Mortensen © 1980 by Alice H. Mortensen. Used by permission of granddaughter Linda Ladd.

Grateful appreciation is expressed to my good friend, Craig Stoner, a staff assistant at New Day, Inc., for his tireless efforts to secure written permission for many of the entries in this book. Any inadvertent errors, however, are the responsibility of the author.

New Day, Inc.

The possibility of experiencing new life in each new day is the underlying theme in this book. I have the joy of seeing people experience a new day in my work at New Day, Inc. The new day theme points to the power of God to bring new life into being. Thus, New Day, Inc. (NDI) is a Christian ministry that serves those who need this newness. New Day, Inc. offers marriage and family therapy, a one-to-one friendship program (Operation Daybreak) for a troubled youth or child, a community outreach program that offers aid to disadvantaged families, a ministry to youths in detention centers, summer camping for youths, prison ministries, a residential program for men in need of rehabilitation, the teaching of parenting classes, financial counseling and other services.

It has been serving portions of Western Pennsylvania since its beginnings in 1978. The ministry began in Johnstown, Pa.

and is now serving in four locations: Johnstown, Windber, Somerset and Altoona.

New Day, Inc. is a faith ministry that is supported by the freewill contributions of caring individuals, churches and church organizations, business and industry, civic and employee groups. NDI receives no federal, state or agency-type support.

Gifts to sustain this ministry are needed and greatly appreciated. All gifts to NDI are tax-deductible as allowed by IRS regulations.

If you would like to have copies of this book sent to members of your family, friends or associates, you may request the same by writing to any of the four addresses for New Day, Inc. Please enclose a donation of $10 to the ministry of New Day, Inc. for each book requested.

New Day, Inc.

109 South St.
Johnstown, PA 15901
(814) 535-8202

1428 Graham Ave.
Windber, PA 15963
(814) 467-4499

137 Missoura St.
Somerset, PA 15501
(814) 445-7557

1507 12th St.
Altoona, PA 16601
(814) 949-9210

Other materials by Noah Martin include:

Books

Beyond Renewal
A Vision For a New Day

Booklets

Believing In the Cross of Jesus
Believing In the Resurrection of Jesus
How to Deal With Problems, Problems, Problems
The Therapy of Thanksgiving
Finding the Comfort of God
Peace For Your Life
Abiding in Christ

Cassette Tape

"The Power to Change: Your Choice"